# Animal Legs

by Mary Holland

Legs and feet come in many shapes, numbers, and sizes. They are used to paddle, jump, cling, dig, warn others, catch food and even taste food! The way an animal's legs and feet look can tell you a lot about how it lives.

Like all insects, backswimmers have three pairs of legs. Each pair of legs has a different job. Backswimmers catch prey with their two front legs, hold the prey tight with their two middle legs, and row through the water with their two flat, hairy, hind legs.

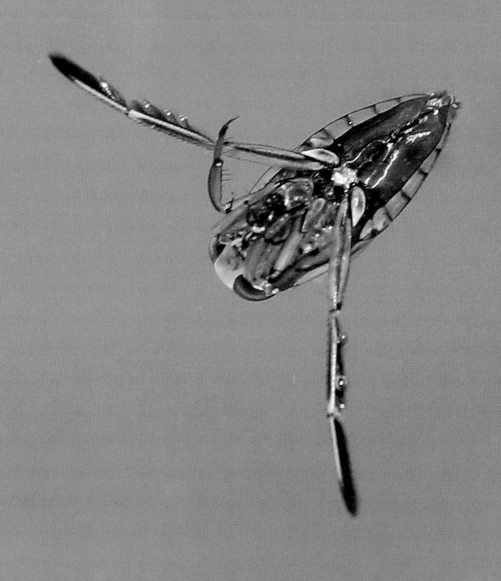

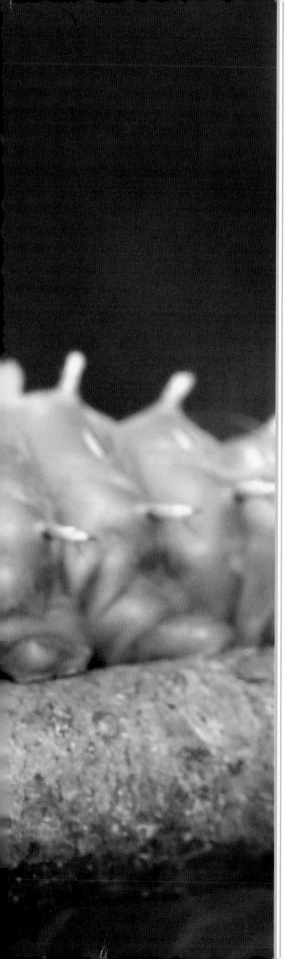

Caterpillars may look like they have a lot of legs, but only the first three pairs are true legs. The others are called prolegs. True legs have several sections and often have a claw at the tip. Prolegs have tiny, curved hooks (crochets) that act like suction cups. These hooks allow caterpillars to climb smooth surfaces like plant stems and leaves. The true legs on this cecropia moth caterpillar are green. The feet on its prolegs are blue—can you find them?

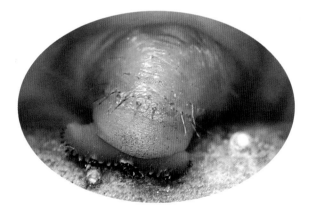

When a caterpillar turns into a moth or a butterfly, it keeps its six true legs, but not its prolegs.

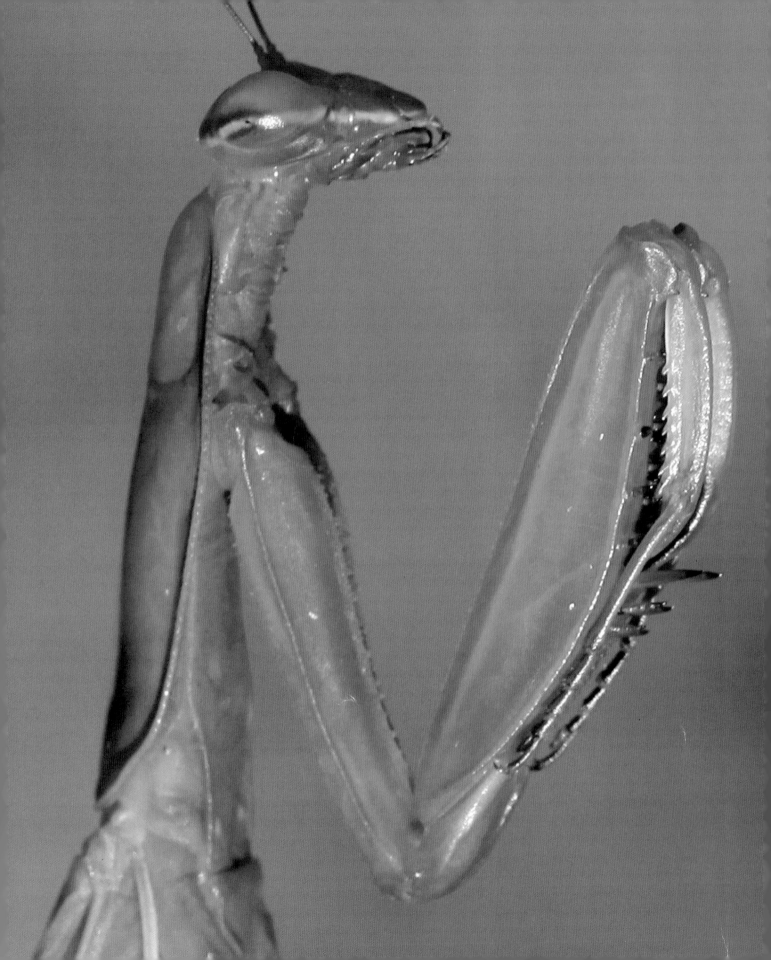

This insect is called a praying mantis because its two front legs are bent and held together which makes it look like the mantis is saying its prayers.

Praying mantises are predators and eat other insects like crickets, grasshoppers and flies. They use their front legs to grasp their prey. The spines on these legs interlock when they grab an insect, making it almost impossible for the insect to escape.

Most spiders and many
insects, such as butterflies,
houseflies, and mosquitoes,
taste with their feet! When
a spider or insect lands on a
flower, leaf, or animal, its feet
taste it. The spider or insect
knows if it has landed on
something that is good to eat
or drink.

Most frogs that live in water, like this green frog, have webbed hind feet. The webbing between the toes turns a frog's foot into a flipper. Do you ever wear flippers when you go swimming? You can swim much faster with flippers on your feet, and so can frogs! With webbing on their hind feet and strong hind leg muscles, a frog can swim very far, very fast.

Most frogs that live on land have hind feet that are not webbed.

Some frogs that live on land have special, round toe pads that are very sticky.

Many of the frogs that have them, like this gray treefrog, live in the woods. These toe pads help them climb up high in shrubs and trees.

Turtles that live in ponds and streams often have webbed feet to help them swim. They also have long claws, or toenails, which help them climb up river banks, stumps and floating logs where they like to bask in the sun.

Turtles also use their legs and claws to dig holes where they can lay eggs.

Birds that hunt animals (birds of prey) have strong claws, called talons, for grabbing their prey.

Talons are very, very sharp. Hawks, falcons, owls, and eagles use their talons to catch rabbits, mice, fish, and many other animals. They then hold their prey in their talons while they tear it into small pieces with their beak.

The feet of a ruffed grouse look different in the winter than they do in the summer. In the fall, a grouse grows special, tiny flaps (pectinations) on both sides of each toe.

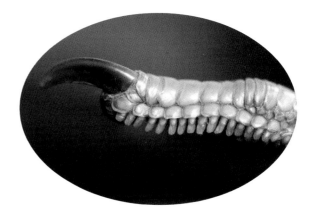

These flaps make the grouse's feet bigger and help it walk on top of the snow, just like snowshoes keep people from sinking deep into the snow.

Ruffed grouse often perch on icy tree branches to eat buds. These flaps help it grip the ice and not slip off the branch. In the spring, when the snow and ice are gone, these flaps fall off, but they will grow back in the fall.

Many people don't like striped skunks because they have a smelly spray, but skunks usually don't spray unless they are very scared. Even then, they usually give a warning before they spray. Skunks announce that they are about to spray by stamping their feet. Can you stamp your feet like a skunk?

When an animal sees a skunk doing this, it knows to turn and run away if it doesn't want to get sprayed. Usually the animal leaves, but if it doesn't, the skunk points its rear end at the animal, lifts its tail, squeezes its scent glands, and covers the animal with a smelly spray.

River otters spend a lot of time in the water. Much of the time they are catching fish, frogs and turtles to eat. In order to catch their food, otters must be able to swim very fast. All four of their feet are webbed, with flaps of skin between the toes. Like frogs, ducks, and other animals with webbed feet, river otters can move quickly through the water.

Moles are small, furry animals that dig tunnels underground. The front feet of a mole look and act like little shovels. They are short, but very strong and their legs have lots of muscles. When they dig a tunnel, moles paddle their feet through the soil just as if they were swimming.

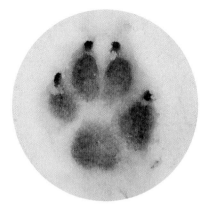

Some animals, like birds, cats, and dogs, walk on their toes.

Other animals, such as deer and moose, walk on their toe nails.

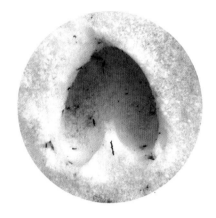

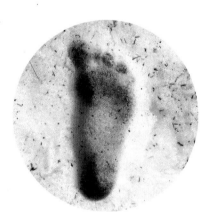

Animals like raccoons, bears, and humans walk on their whole foot.

While humans may not move as fast as most four-legged animals that run on their toes or nails, we can stand up and walk, run, and jump on only two legs. What else can you do with your legs and feet?

# For Creative Minds

## Special Feet

Most, but not all, animals have feet. Animals that don't have feet, like this milk snake, have strong muscles in their abdomen that grip the earth beneath their belly when they move.

The toe flaps (pectinations) of ruffed grouse that live in northern areas with long winters and deep snow are twice as long as those of grouse living further south.

In just one minute, a mole can dig a tunnel as long as your two hands put together. It uses its front feet to dig with while its hind feet kick the loose dirt above the ground.

A woodpecker spends a lot of time clinging to the bark of trees while it drills holes with its beak to reach insects or make nesting holes. Many birds have three toes pointing forward and one toe pointing backwards. Woodpeckers have two toes in front and two toes in back (zygodactyl feet), which gives them a much better grip on tree trunks and branches.

Some mammals, like the fisher, have scent glands (dark spots on pads) on their feet. They leave a little scent of themselves with every step they take.

# What Legs Can Do

Match the descriptions on the right with the animals on the left. Answers are below.

white-tailed deer

honey bee

red squirrel

mallard duckling

spider

dragonfly

1. My legs are a weapon. I kick predators so they'll leave me alone.

2. I use my legs to swim. Webbed toes help me paddle in the water.

3. My legs can catch my next meal. I have three pairs of legs

4. My legs and feet help me grip the bark and scurry up a tree.

5. I use all eight legs to walk along my web. My feet can taste food.

6. My legs have small pouches. I carry pollen from flower to flower.

Answers: 1: white-tailed deer. 2: mallard duckling. 3: dragonfly. 4: red squirrel. 5: spider. 6: honey bee.

# Match the Foot to the Animal

Match these feet with the animals they belong to. What can you tell about the animals by their feet? What do you think these animals use their feet for? Answers are below.

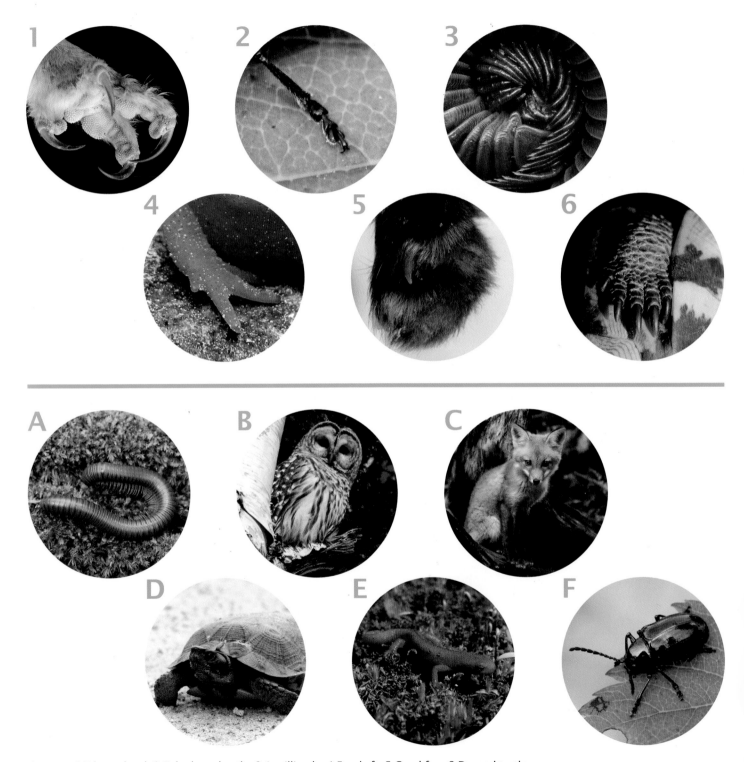

Answers: 1-B barred owl, 2-F dogbane beetle, 3-A millipede, 4-E red eft, 5-C red fox, 6-D wood turtle

# Fun Facts

Opossums have a special "thumb" on each hind foot that can touch each of the toes on the same foot. This opposable thumb helps an opossum grasp branches and climb.

Humans have opposable thumbs on our hands. Can you touch the your thumb to the tips of your other fingers on the same hand? Imagine how hard it would be to climb a tree, brush your teeth or eat a sandwich if you didn't have opposable thumbs.

Porcupines eat bark and spend a lot of time in trees. Their feet help them climb up tree trunks and out onto limbs where they eat leaves and buds. The claws on a porcupine's foot are curved and grip the bark of a tree very well. The pad on the bottom of each foot is bumpy. These bumps help the foot hold onto the bark of a tree.

A beaver's front feet are small and not webbed. Beavers use them to hold mud, sticks and stones, but they don't paddle with them. A beaver's hind feet are very large and have webbing between the toes. When a beaver swims, it paddles through the water with its hind feet and steers with its tail. Each hind foot has two nails, which are split. A beaver uses these nails to comb leaves, sticks, insects, and snarls out of its fur. A beaver uses the nails on all four feet to spread oil on its coat to make it waterproof.

All spiders spin silk, and their legs help guide the silk as they make things with it. Most spider legs end with two claws. With help from their legs some spiders weave silk webs, wrap prey, make egg sacs and create silk nurseries for their young. A spider's eight legs and feet help it capture food, weave silk, stalk prey, and climb up plant stems.

To Ginny, Joan, Erin, and Sandra—my good friends and fellow naturalists who never fail to inspire me.—MH

Thanks to Max Capurso for modeling for the snowshoe photograph.

Thanks to Roger Wrubel, Sanctuary Director at Mass Audubon's Habitat Education Center & Wildlife Sanctuary, for verifying the accuracy of the information in this book.

Library of Congress Cataloging-in-Publication Data

Names: Holland, Mary, 1946- author.
Title: Animal legs / by Mary Holland.
Description: Mount Pleasant, SC : Arbordale Publishing, [2016] | Audience:
  Ages 4-8. | Includes bibliographical references.
Identifiers: LCCN 2016019114 (print) | LCCN 2016020081 (ebook) | ISBN
  9781628558432 (english hardcover) | ISBN 9781628558449 (english pbk.) |
  ISBN 9781628558463 (english downloadable ebook) | ISBN 9781628558487
  (english interactive dual-language ebook) | ISBN 9781628558456 (spanish
  pbk.) | ISBN 9781628558470 (spanish downloadable ebook) | ISBN
  9781628558494 (spanish interactive dual-language ebook) | ISBN
  9781628558463 (English Download) | ISBN 9781628558487 (Eng. Interactive) |
  ISBN 9781628558470 ( Spanish Download) | ISBN 9781628558494 (Span.
  Interactive)
Subjects: LCSH: Leg--Juvenile literature. | Animal locomotion--Juvenile
  literature. | Anatomy--Juvenile literature. | Adaptation
  (Biology)--Juvenile literature.
Classification: LCC QL950.7 .H586 2016 (print) | LCC QL950.7 (ebook) | DDC
  591.47/9--dc23
LC record available at https://lccn.loc.gov/2016019114

Translated into Spanish: *Patas de los animales*
Keywords: adaptations, feet, legs, movement
Lexile® Level: NC 1020L
Animals in the order they appear in the book: red-legged grasshopper (cover), snowy egret, backswimmer, cecropia caterpillar, praying mantis, hairstreak, green frog, gray treefrog, painted turtles, red-shouldered hawk, ruffed grouse, striped skunk, North American river otter, hairy-tailed mole.

Bibliography:

Education Department. *Two Legs, Four Legs, Six Legs, More!* National Aquarium. 2012. Web.

Holland, Mary. *Naturally Curious: A Photographic Field Guide and Month-By-Month Journey Through the Fields, Woods, and Marshes of New England.* North Pomfret, VT: Trafalgar Square Books, 2010.

Manufactured in China, May 2016
This product conforms to CPSIA 2008
First Printing

Arbordale Publishing
Mt. Pleasant, SC 29464
www.ArbordalePublishing.com